MANIPULATION:

SECRETS OF MANIPULATION AND DARK PSYCHOLOGY.

Defense and Attack Guide

Rick Mulville

ISBN: 978-1-80186-099-4

Furthermore, the information that can be found within the pages described forthwith shall be considered both accurate and truthful when it comes to the recounting of facts. As such, any use, correct or incorrect, of the provided information will render the Publisher free of responsibility as to the actions taken outside of their direct purview. Regardless, there are zero scenarios where the original author or the Publisher can be deemed liable in any fashion for any damages or hardships that may result from any of the information discussed herein.

Additionally, the information in the following pages is intended only for informational purposes and should thus be thought of as universal. As befitting its nature, it is presented without assurance regarding its prolonged validity or interim quality. Trademarks that are mentioned are done without written consent and can in no way be considered an endorsement from the trademark holder.

Table of Contents

Introduction

What if I told you that you can get whatever you want in life? You wouldn't believe me, right? But it's true. You do have the power to get what you want. One of the biggest obstacles that stand in your way is other people, right? So in this book, I will show you how to undermine and get around other people with dark psychology.

The term "dark" puts people off. It is generally associated with evil. While the techniques in this book can certainly be used for evil, they are not necessarily evil in and of themselves. It all depends on how you choose to use these super powerful techniques of influence and mind control. The secrets contained in this book are not light; you can use them to gain control over anyone that you want. They are foolproof and very powerful. When you decide to use these methods, you will experience very quick and successful results.

You hold a great deal of power when you learn these methods. You will have access inside the minds of others. Once you gain this access, you will be able to do whatever you want with someone's mind. You can convince someone to believe you when you're lying. You can get someone to do what you want. You can even shatter someone mentally and emotionally, thus successfully winning a psychological war once and for all.

This book covers some topics that are extremely advanced. Practice makes perfect and it is certainly important to practice these tactics in order to get them right. You don't want to mess up and show someone that you are actively trying to manipulate them. Being covert is key to the success of the skills covered in this book. However, sometimes you need to run before you walk, so it is perfect if you want to start with the more advanced tactics covered in this book.

First, we will cover secrets of human psychology which very much help you learn how to employ the methods contained in this book.

You must understand the inner working of the human mind in order to manipulate it. You can't hope to manipulate people if you don't understand how their minds work. A good manipulator is a home expert in psychology. This book will show you how most people operate and how to use basic human psychology to your advantage.

Next, we will delve into the good stuff. We will talk about how to crush enemies. Psychological warfare is an ancient method of using human psychology to destroy enemies. Psychological warfare is useful to know because it really works. But it is also perfectly legal. You will be able to get away with psychological warfare, whereas using violence could land you in prison.

We will also cover Dark NLP. NLP is a very successful way to make other people like you and do what you want. Dark NLP takes NLP a step further by teaching how to use NLP methods to get people to do bad things for you or to trick people and deceive people easily. Since NLP really works, dark NLP is a surefire way to wage dark psychology on people.

CBT is another thing that we cover. CBT is cognitive behavioral therapy and it is a special favorite of therapists because it works so well. You can use dark CBT to convince people to change their behavior and think against their will. You can mold people into what you want using dark CBT.

We wouldn't be a good dark psychology book if we didn't cover the topics of manipulation and persuasion. Getting what you want in this world is important. Often people will say no to you. But if you know how to manipulate and persuade, you can easily get people to always say yes.

Mind control is a last resort for dealing with people who won't do what you want. Kamikaze mind control is a great way to get people to bend to your will and become whom you want.

If you want to lie, the number one problem is getting caught. Getting caught in a lie is a terrible way to lose credibility and to damage your relationships. You may even lose loved ones if you are caught lying. Learning how to deceive even a perceptive FBI interrogator will help you avoid ever being detected while lying. We will also teach you how to always cover your tracks so that you can get away with anything that you do.

Getting people to like you is the best way to get a leg up in the world. You won't do well or be successful if people don't like you.

You can use a variety of psychological tricks and methods to make people like you.

Finally, we'll talk about erecting a good façade. If you want to use dark psychology, you can't be obvious about it. Remember how I said that being covert and discreet is essential? You need to learn how to create a façade that makes people like you and that hides what you are really up to.

Are you ready to dive in now? You will possess powerful, advanced knowledge about human psychology and how to manipulate people and gain control of their minds. What you choose to do with this information is up to you. But you will certainly gain a lot of power with this knowledge.

What Is Dark Persuasion?

Persuasion is the act of prevailing over another person to believe something by the use of various reasoning or arguments. There is ethical persuasion and dark persuasion. The difference between these two types of persuasions is the intent. An ethical persuader may try to convince another person to do something without giving much thought to certain tactics. They may do this without ulterior motive or real understanding of the person they are trying to persuade. This particular persuader may be concerned with creating good for many people like a diplomat negotiating against the war. This is the persuader known to be ethical.

On the other hand, there is a dark persuader. This particular individual is well aware of the bigger picture. He has a full understanding of the person he is trying to persuade, what motivates them, and to what extent they can go for their tactic to be successful. A dark persuader is not concerned with how moral their manipulation is, doing the right thing is not their motivation. When a dark persuader identifies a thing they want, they devise a way to get it and do not care who gets hurt in the process. Their goal is to always get what benefits them no matter the cost.

When is Persuasion used?

Persuasion is used every day by every person in various ways. Children use persuasion to get their parents to do for them what they want or buy for them something. In intimate relationships, partners persuade each other in order to get what each wants. Persuasion in business is common. A business owner needs to persuade his or her customers to buy their services or products. Writers also use persuasion to pull people towards buying their books. Persuasion is common and can be ethical or unethical depending on the intent of the person doing the persuasion.

Different techniques are used to persuade individuals. These techniques can be used for both dark persuasion and ethical persuasion. The outcome of any form of persuasion is to get your opponent, partner or audience to do as you wish them to do so that you benefit. It becomes unethical persuasion when the only person that stands to gain is the one doing the persuasion. When it is only one person gaining, it means it is getting what a person wants at the expense of the other person.

Persuasive Techniques used in Business.

As earlier said, persuasion is common in every field. If a person is a certain outcome, they may result in persuading the other person for the same. Some of the techniques individuals use to persuade others whether ethically or unethically are:

Resonating with the other person's problems – every person has one problem or another. Service providers and manufacturers design their products with this knowledge in mind. They understand in order to sell their service or product; they must be solving a certain problem. If you want someone to do something for you, you should also appeal to their emotional side. People that want to persuade others for selfish gains make sure that they understand the emotional problems and appeal to it. Psychopaths that persuade to take advantage are able to recognize the emotional side of their victims through cognitive empathy.

When you show a person that you understand their problems, you will easily get them to do what you want them to do. Whether it is a product you are selling or a service, a person wants to find a solution to their problem. On the other hand, a person that feels they have a friend in another one that is pretending to empathize with their situation is likely to please their empathizer by doing as they ask.

If you are a writer, you must put yourself in the shoes of your readers. You must offer your readers what solves their problems by making them see that you understand them. If you resonate with your audience with their problems, it is likely that they will resonate with you in your solutions.

Understanding your audience is key to being able to persuade them. If you are a businessman looking at selling a product, you must ask yourself some of the following questions in order to resonate with your clients. These questions are dependent on the service or product you sell. For instance:

-     How is the view of the world towards your audience's finances?

-     How is the emotional view of the world towards your audience?

-     How is the world's view towards your audience spiritually?

-     How is the world's view to your audience physically?

In response to this, a business person may see the world in relation to their customer as:

-     The purchasing power of his target customer is average

-     Your customers are struggling to make ends meet

-     Spiritually, your customers wish to get value for money

-     Physically, your clients are struggling with health issues

Being able to understand your audiences as a businessman will enable you persuade them to buy your services or products. A psychopath understands this principle well and ensures to form a pretentious friendship with their potential victim in order to make it easy to persuade them.

Use facts or dates to persuade – not everything is emotional. Whether you want to persuade someone ethically or unethically especially in business, use of analytical information and data goes a long way. The person doing the persuasion understands his or her audience and uses the tools at their disposal to get what they want. For instance, if a person wants to persuade another to buy a product that they know is not good, they may use bogus figures to convince their potential client. Not all products are directed at solving emotional problems. The use of data strengthens a person's pitch while persuading another.

The best way to persuade a person to buy a product is to come up with irrefutable evidence that your product or service is the best. A person that is ethical will produce genuine evidence while an unethical person will come up with fake evidence that will be convincing.

Illustrate social proof – this is the psychological evidence where a person assumes the actions of another as an attempt to demonstrate right behavior in a particular situation. What this means is that when a person is making a decision, they want other people to see it as the best decision. These people will include people we hold in high regard, potential clients or random strangers.

In the recent past, social proof has been in the form of recommendations from social influencers, testimonials from customers as well as social share count. People with ethical intentions in their persuasion will give genuine feedback from their customers. They do not hide their bad reviews from potential customers instead they provide both the good and the bad so that a customer makes an informed decision. However, individuals that are out to use unethical persuasion may fabricate customer reviews. They may even go ahead and delete any genuine reviews from customers in case they reflect badly on them. All this is done in an effort to persuade customers to buy what they are selling with the belief it is good.

Use of tine to connect emotionally – when talking to prospective clients, a person may use a friendly tone. Your tone can show interest in the needs of a customer or can show a don't care attitude towards the customer. Your tone can make a person yield to your persuasion or not. After studying the situation, a psychopath will know the type of tone to use to persuade their victim into yielding into their demands. This is the same even in business, a salesman must study the mood of his audience and use the appropriate tone to persuade them. In relationships as well, when a partner needs something from the other, they observe their partner's mood and know the appropriate tone to use if they hope to persuade them.

It is also important for a person to be mindful of their tone. It is possible for a tone to insult or encourage. Psychopaths understand this all too well and are careful to use a tone that is appealing to their audience. They will use polite words and show patience with their potential victims in order to get what they want. The same tactic should also be applied in ethical persuasions.

When persuading whether ethical or unethical. It is important to take time and ensure all objectives are covered. Do not be in a hurry when you are trying to persuade someone. Patience is key. Psychopaths are never in a hurry with their victims. You may be surprised to know that con men are the most patient people. This is because for their scheme to work, they must feign interest in the victim and make them feel at ease. Equally, a business person must be patient when trying to persuade a potential client to buy their service or product.

Use of rhetorical questions – a person is not supposed to answer a rhetorical question but it is meant to provoke the thoughts of the other person. Psychopaths know to effectively persuade their victims, they ask rhetorical questions. In business, rhetorical questions are thought-provoking. They cause someone to think outside the box or influence someone towards the outcome you desired of them.

Writers to persuade their readers are known to open their first paragraphs with a hook. When doing a sales pitch or presentation, you need to hook your audience in. Starting with a hook is the best way to do it. Similarly, a psychopath knows to get his victim interested, he or she must start their persuasion tactic with an enticing prospect. This, before a person presents other facts is the first thing towards persuading a person.

Start with small requests and move on to big ones. This is a tactic used in all forms of persuasions. You don't begin by asking for something very big instead you begin with small things. Once the person has yielded, then you can move on to bigger things.

Make short and to the point statements – a complicated narrative is confusing to the other person. Psychopaths assume their victims know nothing and they need to make them understand. They will use precise statements that are clear and easy to understand. The same applies to business. If you need to persuade a person to make a certain decision, using precise short statements that are clear will convince them faster than a lot of narratives.

Persuasion is an art. It begins with a person understanding what outcome they are hoping for and formulating the best strategy for successful persuasion. The outcome is what determines the persuasion technique to use.

Other persuasive techniques used

Persuasion is used to convince a person about something they would not have considered otherwise. Advertisements are one-way persuasion techniques are employed. The same techniques used to sell a good thing can be used to manipulate a person. There are other ways a person can persuade you, these include:

Appealing to authority – if you are trying to persuade a person into doing something, using important people or experts to pass your point across is very convincing. When you reliably research, you can make your argument very convincing and sway your audience. For instance, a person can say:

Example - The former first lady Michele Obama has said the only way to eradicate obesity among children is getting rid of junk food from vending machines.

Example – according to a recent study, watching tv reduces stress causing a reduction in the risk of heart diseases.

- Both these statements whether true or falsified can convince a person that what is being said is true because a person has appealed to authority. Dark persuasion can also appeal to authority in order to convince their victim to do as they wish for them to do.

Appeal to reason – people are easily convinced when a person uses logic to persuade them. For instance, a person would say:

A bar of chocolate contains 300 calories and 20 grams of sugar. That is not so bad! You can still enjoy you're a bar of chocolate every day because it is within your caloric limit.

- Although that statement is not entirely true, a person that wants you to push their sales yet they know it is not healthy for you will use it to persuade you. People tend to trust where there are figures believing the information to be authentic. This tactic is widely used to manipulate individuals to do as other wishes.

Empathize or appeal to emotion – making a person feel sad, angry or happy can help you persuade them. For instance:

A person may say to you that your donation is important because it may feed a hungry child for a day or

If you do not donate, a child will go hungry and die and you will be part of the reason.

- Both those statements serve to persuade an individual to make a contribution. The first one appeals to the person to empathize with a situation while the second statement serves to guilt-trip the individual. Both statements are aimed at getting a contribution. However, one is used in an ethical way while the other is unethical or dark persuasion.

Appealing to Trust – if a person trusts and believes you, it becomes easier to persuade them. Most psychopaths make sure their victims trust them and that is how they are able to persuade them. It is almost impossible to persuade a person that doesn't trust you. Trust is important if one is to be convinced. For instance:

If a person seems to be doing well financially and tells you to invest in something, they may say to trust them that's how they began. They know you are desperate to have financial stability and because you may know their story, you will believe them.

If this person is genuine, then you are likely to have made a good investment. However, embezzlers, on the other hand, are people that are also trusted by those that invest with them. They convince their victims to invest in a certain thing because it pays. You trust them because they seem to have a good reputation and seem to know what they are doing. Unfortunately, this person is appealing to your trust to invest your hard-earned money but they swindle you. This is dark persuasion in play. All the people that have had their funds embezzled trusted their embezzlers.

Plain folk – manipulators know to persuade their victims or audience, they must appear to be the average kind of a person. For instance, politicians use persuasion tactics to get voters. He or she may just say:

"I am an average person. I relate to the suffering we have endured under the current leadership and it is time we changed the narrative. I have grown up with you in this neighborhood, I have faced the same challenges and therefore I am the best candidate."

- This kind of appeal is to show that a politician is an average person just like the voters. The politician wants the voters to believe he can relate with them because he is one of the – ordinary. Whether the information is true or not, whether the politician just wants votes and will do nothing or not, he will manage to convince the electorate through such statements.

Bandwagon – this is the presumption that everyone trusts it, so it must be good or true. This is very common in advertisements. For instance:

A company advertising its brand of toothpaste may claim that 2 out of every American household use this product. It has been trusted by families for generations to offer the best in cavity protection.

- No one wants to have cavities. If you are convinced that that product is the number one bestseller and the majority of the people trust it, you will definitely buy it. It is important to remember that some of these statistics are not true. To push sales of a product regardless of if the product does perform as indicated, companies can come up with untruths.

- Bandwagon is also a tactic used majorly on social media. If a person notices many likes regarding a particular product, they rush out to buy it. The assumption is that if many like it, it must be good. However, it is possible that it is the advertisement that was well crafted and not the product.

Rhetorical Question – when a person wants to persuade another one, they will use rhetorical questions. For instance, if a person is promoting a skin care regiment, they may ask their audience, "Who wouldn't like to have fair glowing skin?" the answer is obvious. It provokes the person to think and wish to have flawless skin and end up buying the product.

Another person may want to sell you shares knowing very well that the share value is likely to drop. They show you convincing figures and ask you, "wouldn't you want to make money?" Even the richest person in the world wants to make more money! This kind of tactic will end up convincing you to invest even though it could be a wrong investment.

Elements of Persuasion

Persuasion is about selling; selling a story, a product or a service. Everyone has been persuaded in one way or another. You may have been persuaded to take up a certain job, get married, buy something or believe in something bigger than you thought you could. Probably you are dating currently, it took persuasion to get you to go on a first date or another and so forth. The person has persuaded you to a point that you are intrigued to know more about them.

Each day, a person is persuading another to do things that will directly benefit them. That is selling. Selling does not have to be in monetary value but it can be a belief. Selling in this sense is convincing someone on something they believe they want or they don't know if they want or selling them something that they must have.

For instance, when girl scouts come knocking at your door to sell you cookies, you don't need them but you want them and they will persuade you to buy them.

Persuasion can be viewed in various ways. A person can use persuasion for their own selfish gains or they can use persuasion ethically for the mutual benefit of the parties involved. Either way, the elements to persuade a person are the same but the motives or intent may differ. There are various elements to persuasion that lead to effective communication. Below, we discuss each element in detail.

Elements of persuasion for effective communication

The Communicator

The communicator is the person that is trying to persuade the listener. He or she must be able to deliver the message without interruptions. According to experts, for a message to be effective, it is not what is said but how it is said. A communicator to be able to persuade the listener, he or she must make sure the message is delivered in such a way that the listener interprets it just as the communicator intended it to be.

To do this effectively, the communicator must have believable credibility, should be trustworthy, have a personality that is likable and is patient. When a communicator lacks any of these things, they are not likely to be listened to. Individuals that are good at persuading whether ethically or unethically, have these qualities about them.

Content of the message

The message the communicator is passing to the listener must be of interest to them. A communicator must research their listener, know what they need or their problem and appeal to it. When a communicator identifies with the listener's problem, they offer solutions. This is what the listener wants and by doing it, the communicator will win the listener over.

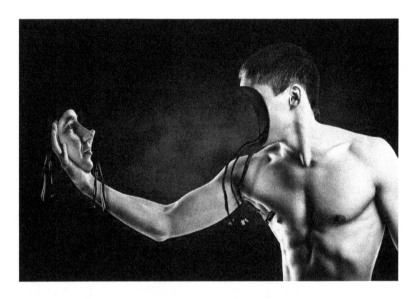

The channel of communication

If you are communicating with a person, you obviously expect a response. The channel you choose to deliver the message matters. Choose a channel that gives you the best response and in the quickest manner. If you need to make a call so that you get an immediate response, then do that. Understand your audience so that you can use the best communication channel to persuade them.

The listeners or Audience

To know if the communicator is doing a good job of persuasion, the determinants are the audience. When delivering a message, the listener's communicator must observe the nonverbal clues that the listener gives. For instance, see if the listener is focused on your message by leaning in to show interest, smiling, shaking their head, or even sitting up. Other cues that would show interest is if the listener is asking questions and if you are selling a product, asking to buy.

The Main Elements of Persuasion – Pathos, Ethos, and Logos

Aristotle broke down the elements of persuasion into three. These included the pathos, logos, and ethos. Logos refers to logic, ethos is ethics and pathos is the emotional connection.

Logos

Logos is the words and the reasons you have for your argument. When persuading a person, it is important to have all everything fit together before you start passing on the information. Ensure your argument is coherent by thinking it through before you begin to talk. To effectively persuade, organize your points in a sequence that starts from the general to the particular or from the beginning to the end. Let every subsequent point build on the previous one so your argument is persuasive.

Ethos

Ethos in persuasion is in reference to the ethics of the communicator. Character, credibility, and believability matters to your audience as a communicator. To persuade effectively, you must increase your credibility towards your audience during and before you pass on the message. If the listener finds you credible, they are likely to appreciate your argument and advice.

Pathos

The emotional aspect of your communication is pathos. To persuade effectively, you must appeal to the emotional side of your listeners. An increased emotional connection enables them to transform their thinking and take the action that the communicator was hoping for.

Any kind of persuasion is divided into these three elements. Before you persuade a person whether ethically or unethically, you must appeal to logic. Have your facts right or at least have convincing facts. You must be willing to answer any questions the listener may pose to you. This shows them that you know what you are talking about and your information is credible.

The credibility of a communicator to his audience is an important part of persuasion. The listener must believe and trust what you are telling them and it starts with the feeling they can trust you. Your reputation must be good to get a connection to your listener.

Every communication should be geared toward solving a problem. Every person has a problem they want solved. Appealing to the emotions of your audience will enable you to know what their needs are and when you address those needs, you succeed in persuading them.

What Is Covert Emotional Manipulation

Manipulation is a form of intentional influence, characterized as an attempt, by a person or party (the manipulator), to change the behavior of another person or party (the target), typically with a view to achieving a goal in the manipulator's interests.

Two problems remain, however. The first relates to "intended influence." Intent is difficult because it implies responsibility. In actual fact, everyone manipulates everyone around them all the time, even from a young age. It would be wrong to exclude a child's temper tantrum from the umbrella of manipulation, just because they aren't old enough to rationalize their behavior. The same applies to adult temper tantrums, for that matter. Intent, therefore, does not imply conscious behavior – it can also be instinctive. This also allows for the, very real, presence of "naturally manipulative" persons.

The second problem is the disappointingly vague ending: "typically to achieve a goal in the manipulator's interests." Not only is it problematic to define "the manipulator's interests," there is a catch-all ambiguity in the inclusion of "typically." This part serves only to create a normalized idea of manipulation for the purposes of this book and absolutely wouldn't suit a more general definition. After all, how can someone perfectly know their own interests? It is of course possible to successfully manipulate someone, and for the result to still be one's own demise.

How will a manipulator target?

Human beings have various personality traits and types such as warm, passionate, adventurous, loyal and dependable, idealistic, analytical, fun-loving personalities, and many others. Our personality traits are greatly influenced by the biochemical processes ongoing in our bodies. These processes affect how we behave at a given time making some persons to have unpredictable natures and sudden mood swings. Despite all these inconsistencies of the human characters and lives, you still need to learn ways to manipulate and persuade people to get what you want from them.

There are various ways of manipulating a person through persuasion, but you can persuade and influence using your body language and manners of speech respectively. Let us look at some ways to manage and control people like.

Polishing and improving your manipulation strategies

You can clean your skills for effective manipulation of others through mastering the art of public speaking, theatrical displays, creating parallels and correspondences, exhibiting charismatic traits by displaying self-confidence, and learning from the experts.

Applying various methods of manipulation

Getting what you want, will not be possible if you do not know how to use some techniques of manipulating people like using rationality and logic to present your requests to a person, you can even act like a scapegoat and the victim in dangerous situations. These tactics will subconsciously compel your target to give you what you desire without any restraint. Another way to get what you want from a person is by using bribing pattern like offering a person something in exchange for what you want from him or her.

Using Manipulation Techniques on your friends and Acquaintances

Your friends and acquaintances are the best persons to manipulate to get whatever you want. This is because they must have known you and your personality traits and probably despite your faults will continue to stick to you no matter what happens. To achieve this, you will play on their emotions because your friends should have feelings for you and most importantly, they commit to help you and make you happy or comfortable if it is in their power to do it. Play on their conscience by reminding them how you have been helpful in the past, and this will motivate them to offer you whatever you desire.

Theories on successful manipulation

If you get caught, you will not only completely blow your chances at success in that conversation, but you could end up spoiling your reputation. People do not tend to take lightly to this type of situation, as no one likes the idea of being under mind control or brainwashed. In order to avoid this type of disaster, you need to know how to prevent yourself from getting caught. Getting caught can potentially destroy your success at mind control, as well as any relationships you have used this strategy in. When people catch wind that you are attempting to brainwash them, or that you have effectively done so, they will no longer trust you and this mistrust will spread across your network extremely quickly. People do not appreciate being subjected to brainwashing and mind control, and so they do not want to know that someone they have grown to trust is using it on them.

Practice Regularly

The more you practice, the stronger your mind control game is going to become. You want to make sure that you practice often, preferably in every single conversation you have. Even if you don't actually want anything significant from someone, knowing how to get them to say or do certain things you want will help you practice brushing up on your technique. It could be something as easy as getting someone to touch a certain area on their body, say something in particular, or do anything else small and seemingly unimportant. The more you learn to use these techniques to get what you want, the better.

Take Your Time Expanding Your Skill

It cannot be stressed enough how important it is for you to slow down when it comes to practicing your skill. It may seem like a good idea to embrace many of these techniques at once and create a conversation that will help you get what you want, but this can lead to you being caught, quickly. When you put this type of pressure on yourself in a conversation without having any practice, you essentially infuse the conversation with a lot of unnatural and uncomfortable feeling. This is because you are not practiced at the techniques, so you are attempting to recall them and use them on the spot, and you are doing it with too many at once. People are going to see through you, and they are going to catch you in the act.

Start Small

Sometimes, starting with large goals is honorable. When it comes to learning how to use mind control and not getting caught in the process, it is actually inefficient and an excellent way to get caught, quickly. The best thing you can do is start small with things that are seemingly unimportant and irrelevant. This allows you to practice getting people to say yes or do what you want them to do, with very little pressure on the situation overall. Once you get regular results in getting your smaller goals met, you can start practicing getting larger goals met. This will give you the best opportunity to really get natural in your talent and feel confident when it comes to setting out larger goals and accomplishing them.

Be Choosy About Who You Brainwash

It is very important that you are choosy about who you brainwash. Remember, just as you have the opportunity to learn about mind control, so do others. Many people in this day and age are somewhat knowledgeable about the art of mind control. While they may not be masters of it, they may have general knowledge around some tactics such as deceit and manipulation. It is important that you learn to identify those who are more likely to comply with your attempts and those who are more likely to be resistant against mind control.

Be Selective About Phrasing and Actions

It is very important that you are careful about the phrasing you use and the actions you carry when you are using mind control strategies. If you use the wrong phrasing, are too forceful or obvious in your phrasing, or have fidgety or otherwise uncontrolled physical movements, you are more likely to be caught. People will recognize that you have something "off" about you, and will be less likely to trust you or believe you. This means that you are going to ruin your attempts and even more people will be less likely to believe you, because mind control and manipulative types of reputations tend to be exposed and shared on a mass level to prevent other people from becoming manipulated. You need to be very careful in your actions and phrasing, ensuring that you are intentional and that you are behaving in a way that is not going to expose you and let others know what you are doing.

What are some of the motivations of a manipulator?

Your Goals

Given that you're probably already manipulating the people around you to some degree, and being manipulated yourself, the first significant step in achieving effective manipulation is to understand and define your goals. Without defining goals, it's impossible to measure the effectiveness of your current manipulation efforts.

That's not to say you aren't already manipulating with some level of effectiveness. Some people are naturally more manipulative and some people are natural manipulators; however, the two don't always overlap.

Start by thinking about your actions, and your behavior around others. Consider who you view positively at work, or in your social circle, and who you view negatively. Consider, further, how you behave around different people and whether it aligns perfectly to your opinion of them. There is a good chance that it doesn't. In fact, what you are probably already doing is working to earn the good opinion of others who you believe to hold power and influence.

The Goals of Others

While your own goals are the way to measure the success of your efforts, the goals of others are key to forming a successful manipulation strategy.

The key to manipulation is using the goals of others to further your own.

This is the most all-encompassing theory of manipulation and the core of this book's approach to manipulation.

At times, you might hold the cards and can help someone to achieve their own goals. This might be as an employee who possesses vital assets for your boss to achieve success in their role. It might be the case that you are the boss and have the power to promote people... not discounting the power you have to help those people achieve their goals by not firing them.

Having what it takes to help other people achieve their goals gives you inherent value to them.

Understanding goals provides the necessary information for effectively manipulating others. Tools, on the other hand, are the raw materials you have at your disposal for affecting those goals, or the actions taken by others to achieve them.

Power

Power is the ability to help other people succeed. This is an interesting definition because it appears to subvert the normal idea of power as an ability to exert force over others. However, breaking it down, the two are closely related. Having the ability to exert force over others can mean not harming them, not invading their country, not throwing them in jail, not creating laws which negatively impact them; these are all forms of power – the power to help other people succeed is much the same as the power to make other people fail, left unexercised.

These are just positive and negative perspectives of the same thing. The difference is often negligible.

What can you provide people that will help other people achieve their goals? The most obvious thing is extraordinary abilities. Talent is valuable in every aspect of life, from sports competitions, to business, to raising children. If you have talents that other people can use, that's a powerful thing.

Another form of power is authority. The boss gets to decide who is promoted and who is fired. A police officer can arrest you or let you off with a warning, thanks to their legally sanctioned authority. A judge may decide your sentence, based on certain constraints, and their opinion of your nature.

When would I need to manipulate someone

Most times, you may not get what you want in life if you are not ready to take some necessary steps in manipulating other people involved in the process. It is challenging to get what you desire if you are not exactly a careful manipulator. Therefore, you need to learn the necessary steps to use in manipulating people. These steps will surely give you an edge over others because you will know how to appeal to their conscience and mentality without being caught in the act, which may annoy them.

Let us make an analysis of these steps, which involves using some body language expressions and spoken words such as:

Manipulative Looks and Stares

Manipulative looks and stares include wearing of stony faces suggesting displeasure and anger over an incidence or something else, death stares used for intimidating others, sexy looks and stares intended to seduce and lure a person into sexual intimacy, maintaining eye contact with someone without saying anything, rolling of eyes, and many others.

Shouting Down on Someone or Yelling

Insidious or manipulative persons have a way of using these tactics to cow and frighten their victims. Shouting down on someone or yelling at people is a manipulative tendency aimed at making the other person or persons shut up in fear and condescend to your whims and caprices unconsciously. Mostly, bosses use this manipulative tendency or traits in the offices to suppress staffs anger and maintain control or leadership of the firm. In some cases, the staffs are never comfortable whenever the boss is around; everybody whisks away in fear of the next reprimanding action that may happen.

Manipulations by Avoiding you at All Means

When someone avoids or ignores you, by all means, something is possibly wrong in your relationship with that person. This type of attitude manifests in so many ways such as when someone leaves a meeting when you enter, if a person does not acknowledge your presence in a place but acknowledges others, no response to your e-mails, phone calls, and messages. Moreover, if a person avoids eye contact with you, you should know that something is fishing and beware of interactions with such persons.

Preferential or Silent Treatment

One of the ways to manipulate someone to give what you want is by showing them unusual, preferred, or silent treatment. After giving them this type of attention and care, the chances are that they must succumb to your wishes and desires.

Playing on the Emotions

Master manipulators like to play on your emotions to coerce you to give them what they want from you. They know that if they can make you have a feeling for them, you will surely respond to their requests. Therefore, they look for words and expressions that can captivate your feelings and thoughts to give them a leeway into your heart. These manipulators may use words such as "I love you," or anything that can endear them to you. This attitude is to get what they want from you.

Cold Behaviors

This is another good tactic of manipulation, but as the behavior is severe, it does not show up boldly and directly. It manifests subtly and merely displaying aggression and anger as inert frustrations. They are angry but maintaining coolness and calmness. With this mindset, they will surely ignore their responsibilities; they will always arrive late for duties, avoid interacting with other persons, and neglecting to perform their functions purposefully. Additionally, they will be carrying out their jobs poorly and shabbily, unnecessary delays of routines, making sarcastic remarks, acting deaf and dumb to instructions, and many other ugly behavioral traits.

Undue Obstinacy and Difficult

Crafty manipulators are unduly obstinate and challenging. They have a purposeful resolution to be hard and stubborn, always disagreeing with everyone and not condescending to any form of concession. They are crafty negotiators but never arrive at a meaningful agreement or conclusion. This class of persons is very argumentative and quarrelsome. Most of the time, people tend to ignore them in order not to have a headache arguing on simple matters and even quarreling.

Unnecessary Deadline Pressures

Giving unnecessary deadlines is a tactic of some bosses and employers to purposely manipulate their subordinates and even victimize them at the place of work. With this approach, the worker does not have enough time to think and may be under pressure to coordinate himself properly and may miss deadlines and other salient requirements, thereby incurring punishments as the case may be.

Suspending Sex, Food, and other Gratifications

A careful manipulator may in a relationship such as between husband and wife decide to discontinue offering sex, food, and other forms of gratification to their partner to induce or coerce him or her to approve something or agree to do something. It could even be done tactically, to get help, money, and other pleasantries from the spouse.

Unsolicited Treats, Gifts, and Favors

When someone decides to offer you unwanted gifts, treats, and favors, it could portend that such one is looking for a leeway into your life to get something they have been expecting. People usually say, "There is no free lunch anywhere." This saying means that 'nothing goes for nothing' and anything someone gives to you is bait for something 'bigger or equivalent' to what they have given to you.

Manipulation Using Compliments and Flattery

Some persons can manipulate you using unnecessary compliments and flattery, which is intended to get a favor from you. They tend to influence you with their words as they shower you with praises in an attempt to appeal to your conscience and reasoning.

How The Mind Works When It Is Manipulated

When it comes to working with dark manipulation, there are going to be a lot of different methods and techniques that we are able to use in order to get what you want. Remember we are talking about some forms of manipulation that are going to help us to get what we want but may end up harming the other person in the process. This means that they may not be seen as the best options to work with, and you may feel a bit uncomfortable with them if you have not worked in dark manipulation, or even with dark persuasion, in the past.

However, working with these techniques will help you to get the results that you want. They will ensure that the other person you are using as your target will be likely to do the actions or say the things that you would like them to, even though it may not be in their best interests to do so. With that said, let's take a look at some of the different dark manipulation tactics that you are able to use to get someone else to do what you want.

Using isolation to get what you want
The first technique that can be used in mind control includes isolation. Humans are very social creatures. They like to spend some time talking with others, spending time out in public, having close friends, and family, and spending their time in more social situations. When we take this social aspect away from many individuals, it changes the way that they look at life.

Complete physical isolation can be the most powerful. This is when the subject is taken away from all contact with others, including email, social media, phone calls, and physical contact. This is something that has been seen in cults and with other groups. They will often take the person far away from others, and then the only human contact that the person can have is with the captors.

Now, this total physical isolation can be really hard to do, and it is usually only done in really intense situations. If you are just trying to use manipulation, you usually don't want to go through and completely isolate the target. But it is common for a manipulator will typically try to attempt their target mentally as much as possible.

There are a number of methods that the manipulator can use in order to get what they want with the help of manipulation. They could include some seminars that last a week in the country and isolate the person from what they would usually do. They could be a lot of criticisms of the person family and close friends so that the target feels bad and stops seeing them. It could be jealousy that keeps the target at home and limits the amount of influence that anyone outside the manipulator has on the person.

Once the manipulator is able to control the information that goes to the target, they can share information, withhold information, and do anything that they would like in order to continue influencing the target as much as they would like. The target is going to become reliant on the manipulator, and this is how the manipulator is able to work and get what they want from the target. There are no outside influences to tell the target that something is wrong, or that they should watch out, and this ensnares the target even more.

Criticism

The next option to work with when it comes to manipulation is the idea of using criticism. This one is sometimes used with isolated or on its own and it works well because it makes the target feel like they are always doing something that is wrong, and that they are not able to meet the high standards of the manipulator. The criticism can always show up on a variety of topics and could include how they look, who they hang out with, the clothes they wear, their beliefs, and anything that the manipulator thinks will work for this.

When a manipulator decides to use this tactic, they are going to be really good at hiding it behind one of their compliments to the other person. Or they will say something nice and add this little jab at the end of it. This allows them to say all the mean things that they want, and then they can say that the target misheard or misunderstood them and that they hadn't really meant any harm by it. This puts the target in a bad spot because they know the manipulator is being mean to them, but they are the ones who look paranoid and bad in this situation.

The criticism that the manipulator is going to use is often going to be small. They don't want to start out using really big criticisms that are obvious because the target doesn't want to be criticized. If the manipulator starts out with something big, the target is going to fight back and walk away. But when it starts out small with some little comments along the way, it starts to plant a bit of self-doubt, something that the target is going to notice, but they often are not going to fight back against.

They are going to start out with something that may seem like a compliment or like that is going to sound like they are being helpful, but in reality, they are trying to be hurtful in the process. They may say something like, "I didn't know that you liked the color blue. I think you should go with something else." This one is going to have the hidden meaning inside of it that you don't look good in what you are wearing, and your clothes don't look that well.

Or maybe you bring in your favorite outfit to a meeting to make yourself feel better. You are excited and you feel really good about the way that you look and feel in the outfit. But then they are going to say something about how they liked you in some other outfit better. It isn't necessarily mean, but it is said in a manner and at a time that it ends up hurting your feelings in the process.

As time goes on, the type of criticism that is going to be used against the target is going to get worse. And the criticism is going to become quite a bit more obvious as well in order to add in a bit more self-doubt here. This is going to make it so that the target starts to rely on the manipulator a bit more. This is due to the fact that the target is going to feel like they have so many flaws that are hard to ignore, and that the only person who can like them and maybe even loves them, through these flaws will be the manipulator. The fact that the manipulator is still around is a good sign that they care, and this causes the target to be more willing to do what the manipulator asks.

The manipulator is going to find that they are able to use this criticism more of us against them kind of idea if it works better as well. They could even choose to move their criticism to be against the outside world so that they can claim they are more superior.

When this happens, the manipulator is going to claim to their target that they are super lucky that the manipulator is even associating with them. The manipulator will ensure that they are important so that the target is more likely to stick around and do what they want. This alone is meant to be enough if it is done in the right manner so that the target feels lucky just because the manipulator is going to spend time with them.

Alienating the target to get what they want

No one wants to be alienated. They want to feel like they are a part of the group. They want to feel accepted, as they belong, and more. This is never more apparent than when we see a newcomer.

When someone is new to town, or to school, to work, or somewhere else, you will notice that they are trying to figure out how to join into the group and get them to accept them. They are worried that they are going to be alienated, and in order to avoid this, they will do everything in their powers to get others to like them and go along with them, and this is where the manipulator can come in and get what they want.

Newcomers who start to join a new manipulative group are usually going to receive a welcome that is very warm. And they will form a number of new friendships that seem to be much deeper, and have a lot more commitment and meaning behind them compared to anything that they were able to experience in the past.

There are several reasons for this one. First, this gets the target to feel welcome and more indebted to the group, and the manipulator. They are thankful that they have these deep connections, and it is usually easier to get a friend to go along with something that a stranger, so it works to the benefit of the manipulator as well. Add in that the target is scared to be alienated, then they are going to do what they can to keep the relationships going strong.

If there are any doubts that end up arising, later on, these relationships are going to become a powerful tool to ensure they stay with the group. Even if they aren't completely convinced, the target will start to remember their outside world, the world that they had before joining this group, and it is going to seem cold and lonely. They will instead choose to stay with the group, even if there is some manipulation going on.

Simply because of the fact that we do not want to be taken away from the crowd and we don't want others to have anything to do with us, we are going to do what the manipulator wants us too. The fact that humans are very social creatures and like to be included in some kind of group all of the time, it is likely that we are going to give in to these urges to do what the manipulator wants, even if we don't feel like it is the best thing for us.

Using social proof as a form of peer pressure

As we talked about a bit before in the last section, we like it when we are able to be a part of the group. Sometimes we center this around wanting to fit in, and we will follow the rules and do what we can to make sure that we are liked and part of the group. And even when we are more introverted and don't want to be in the group all of the time, we still want to find a group of people we are able to be around and fit in.

The thing is that the manipulator is able to come in here and use the idea of wanting to fit in to help them work against you and get you to do things that you don't want to. They know how much fitting in is going to matter to you as an individual, and they are going to use this to convince their target that they need to act in a certain manner if they want to be able to fit in with others.

When a manipulator wants to work with a group of people with the help of this tactic, such as when you have a cause and want to get some people on your side, then you will use what is known as social proof. This can be almost like brainwashing and can help make it so that the people in the group are going to assume that the actions that others around them are using are the right ones, so they should follow it as well. This is the idea that if everyone else is doing it, then the actions are going to be really justified and it is fine for you to do them as well.

The thing with this one, if the manipulator is successful with what they are doing, then the action that they suggest is not going to matter. This is why it is common for us to find someone who separates out from the group doing actions that may not be seen as acceptable by the rest of society. This can work well any time you are able to find an individual who is feeling some kind of uncertainty about their lives or about what they should be doing. They are going to look around for some guidance on what they should do, and if the manipulator is able to get ahold of them during this time, they are more likely to get their target to go along with whatever they want.

Repetition

This one is going to use the idea of when we do something a bunch of times, it becomes more likely that we are going to get that to turn into a habit and stick. And this is a way that a manipulator is able to control their target. If the manipulator is able to repeat the message over and over again, and they use the same tools when repeating the message, they are more likely to get what they want.

Constant repetition can be a powerful tool of manipulation. It seems like a simple idea but it is going to be really effective. The more times that you are able to repeat your message to the target, and the more you keep things the same each and every time, the more likely it is that they are going to end up doing what you would like.

Fatigue

This method is going to take advantage of someone when they are tired and worn out. When we haven't gotten a lot of sleep recently, and we feel worn down, our decisions are not always going to be the best. Think about how a new mother is going to feel when she is trying to take care of a new baby and hasn't been able to get a lot of sleep done in the last few weeks. Manipulators are either going to wait until their target hasn't been able to get a lot of sleep naturally to ask for something, or they are going to be the ones who create this kind of environment so that the target is low on sleep and energy.

You will find that this can be effective because often we do not have to go for a very long time without sleep before our brains start to go foggy. This is a bad thing when you want to be able to protect yourself from those around you and you want to make sure that you are not manipulated. But for the manipulator, this is really good news. How much sleep deprivation is required to make you feel groggy and tired and will affect your decision-making abilities? According to the Journal of Experimental Psychology, it only takes 21 hours straight of not getting enough sleep before we become more susceptible to the suggestions of others.

This is less than one night of sleep. Many of us have missed this thanks to catching up with work, cramming for a big test, trying to binge watch our favorite shows, staying up with a child who is sick, or for some other reason. Think about how much we have been influenced to do things during that time, and how much worse it could be if someone who was studying and using dark psychology came onto the scene at this time.

While it may not be the best news for your target, it is great news for you. You just need to either force a situation where the person doesn't get a lot of sleep (perhaps take them out for a night on the town and not let them get home before they need to go to work the next day), or wait until you hear they have had a long night and didn't get a lot of sleep. Either way, it is going to end up benefiting you. Once they have missed even one night of sleep, though more is often even better, then you are going to be able to see the results and can start to manipulate them without as much effort.

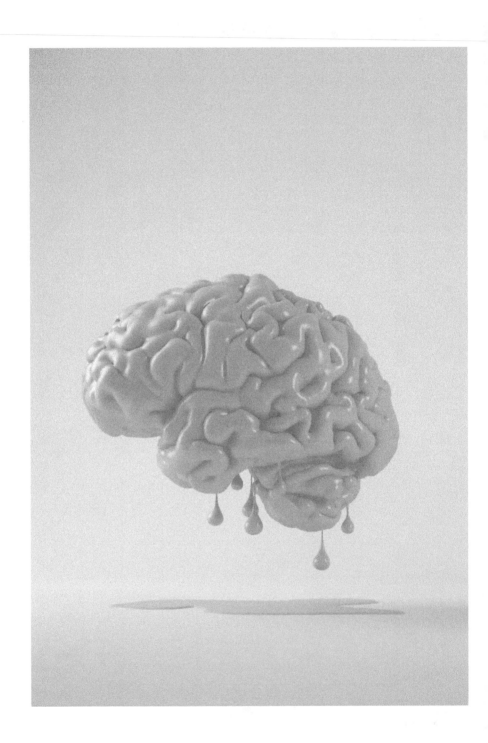

Working to form a new identity in the target

This one is going to take a bit more time to accomplish, and it is not something that you will want to work with if you only plan to work with the individual for a short amount of time. But if you really want to make sure that you are able to manipulate your target as much as possible, and you want to be able to come back to them over and over again to do this, then working on them and helping them to form a new identity may be the option for you. This is something that only skilled manipulators are able to do, but it is going to make a big difference in how you connect and interact with the target.

In this case, the manipulator wants the target to stop being themselves, and they want them to become a robot, someone who is willing to just mindlessly follow their orders. Using all of the methods and the different techniques of mind manipulation that we have talked about in this guidebook, the manipulator is going to try and extract a confession from the target, some kind of acknowledgment that the target believes the manipulator is a good person and doing a good thing. Of course, there can be some slight variations to this, but it is pretty much the same idea no matter how this form is used.

At the beginning of this technique, it may be something that seems pretty insignificant. The manipulator may be trying to get the target to agree that the other members of the group are fun and loving people. It could be the manipulator trying to get the target to agree that at least some of the manipulator's views are valid.

This may seem like a pretty simple thing to work with, but it is priming the target to start thinking with and agreeing with the manipulator on some things. Once they can get the target to agree with them on some of the little things, it is much easier to get them to move on to some of the bigger things. Before you know it, out of the desire to be consistent with what you do and say, you would then find that the target starts to identify themselves as one of the group.

These are just a few of the methods that you are able to use when it comes to working with manipulation in your own life and making sure that you are able to get the target to do what you would like. You will find that manipulation is often going to be a bit darker, and maybe even a bit eviler than the other two methods that we will talk about in this guidebook, and sometimes they may seem a bit advanced for the work that you want to do.

The good news is that as you progress through with dark psychology, you will find that a lot of the techniques that are used in manipulation are going to be very helpful to you when you want to be able to get your way. if you are stuck with some of the other methods that are available, or you find that they are just not cutting it, then using some of the techniques that we have talked about in this chapter are going to be the best option to help you out.

Of course, before you start to use them, consider whether you have formed the right connection with the target ahead of time or not. There are a lot of things that can go wrong when you are using these more advanced techniques, and if you try to use them too early in the process, or before you and the target are ready, then they are not going to work well for you. Once you do the analysis and make sure that you are set and ready to really use them properly, the techniques of manipulation that we have talked about in this chapter are going to prove to be valuable.

Pain Points Of Human Behavior

Grandiose sense of self-importance

Grandiosity is one of the defining traits of a narcissistic person. Grandiosity is more than just vanity or arrogance; it is having an unrealistic sense of superiority. Narcissists believe they are "special and unique and that only other special people can understand them. They only want to be associated as well as associate themselves with other people, places, or things of high status.

Narcissists also believe that no one is better than them and that they should be recognized even when they have done absolutely nothing to earn recognition. They will often lie or exaggerate their talents or achievements. And when they talk about relationships or work, all you will hear is how great they are, how much they contribute, or how lucky people are to have them in their lives.

Sense of entitlement

Since they consider themselves unique and special, narcissistic people always expect to be given favorable treatment. They really believe that they should get whatever they want. They also expect that everyone should automatically comply with all their wishes and the ones who don't in their eyes are useless. And also the ones who dare to ask something in return or entirely defy their will should prepare themselves for outrage, aggression or the cold shoulder.

Needs constant praise and admiration

The sense of superiority in a narcissist is like a balloon that needs a steady stream of recognition and applause to keep it inflated; without it, it gradually loses air. An occasional compliment is not enough. Narcissistic people need constant compliments to feed their ego, and therefore, they tend to surround themselves with people who would do just that. Such kinds of relationships are usually one-sided because it is always about what they get and not what they give. And if they feel like their admirer has reduced their attention and praise or entirely stopped offering it, they would treat that as a betrayal.

Exploits others without guilt or shame

Narcissistic people lack the ability to identify themselves with the feelings of other people, that is, to put themselves into "other people's shoes." This means they lack empathy. Usually, many of the people in their lives are viewed as objects that are there to serve their needs. And as a result of that, they would take advantage of other people without thinking twice as long as they get what they want. While these interpersonal exploitations are usually simply obvious, sometimes they can be outright malicious. Narcissists simply do not possess the ability to think about how people are getting affected by their behaviors. And sometimes, even when it gets pointed out, they would still not get it. Getting their own needs met is the only thing they understand.

Lives in a fantasy world that supports their delusions of grandeur

Reality will never support narcissists' grandiose feelings of themselves; therefore, as a cover, they live in a fantasy world filled with magical thinking, self-deception, and distortion. They have fantasies of glorifying themselves of ideal love, attractiveness; brilliance, power, and unlimited success that make them feel in control and special. Having such fantasies protects them from having feelings of shame and inner emptiness; therefore, opinions and facts that contradict them are either rationalized away or ignored. Anything that poses a threat to their fantasy bubble is usually met with rage or extreme defensiveness.

Frequently belittles, bullies, intimidates or demeans others

Narcissistic and aggressive individuals always feel threatened when they come across a person who appears to have something that they don't have – especially those who have confidence and popularity. They also feel threatened by people who challenge them in any way and the one who aren't submissive towards them. Most times, they would resort to putting these people down as a way to neutralize the threat – contempt is the defense mechanism. This can be done in a dismissive or patronizing way to show how little these people mean to them. And other times, they may choose to go on the attack with threats, bullying, name-calling, and insults to force that person to get back into line.

The types of abusive people

The narcissistic abuser

The narcissist is obsessed with self, they constantly think about self, they worship self, photographs self, promotes self, looks at self and more importantly, they want other people to do all these too. A narcissist is overly concerned with their image, talents, and looks and will do anything no matter the cost to uphold all these. They are also overly concerned with receiving adoration and praise. They love and thrive in the attention they get if any. They are also very charismatic but hate having a charismatic or outgoing partner. They think that this would take attention from them.

A narcissistic abuser is also very inconsiderate, self-absorbed, and very selfish. When socializing with other people, they usually only want to talk about themselves, their accomplishments, talents, pain, and injustices, and if the conversation shifts to another person, they are usually bored and disinterested and only thinks about how to switch the conversation back to themselves.

A narcissistic abuser is the opposite of an emotionally needy abuser for the reason that they can replace a person like a lover at any time with another person. This is because they are only interested in a relationship of any kind only when it benefits them somehow. They may also behave as a good parent to their child for the reason that he perceives the child as their own "extension." This can be termed as indirect narcissism. A narcissist believes that life is all about being "happy" and not about "honor" even if it means obtaining that happiness leaves others unhappy for example, leaving a wife for another woman without caring if the wife and children would feel pain. A narcissist also possesses various other traits of other abusive traits like verbal, physical, emotional, financial, economic, and spiritual abuse.

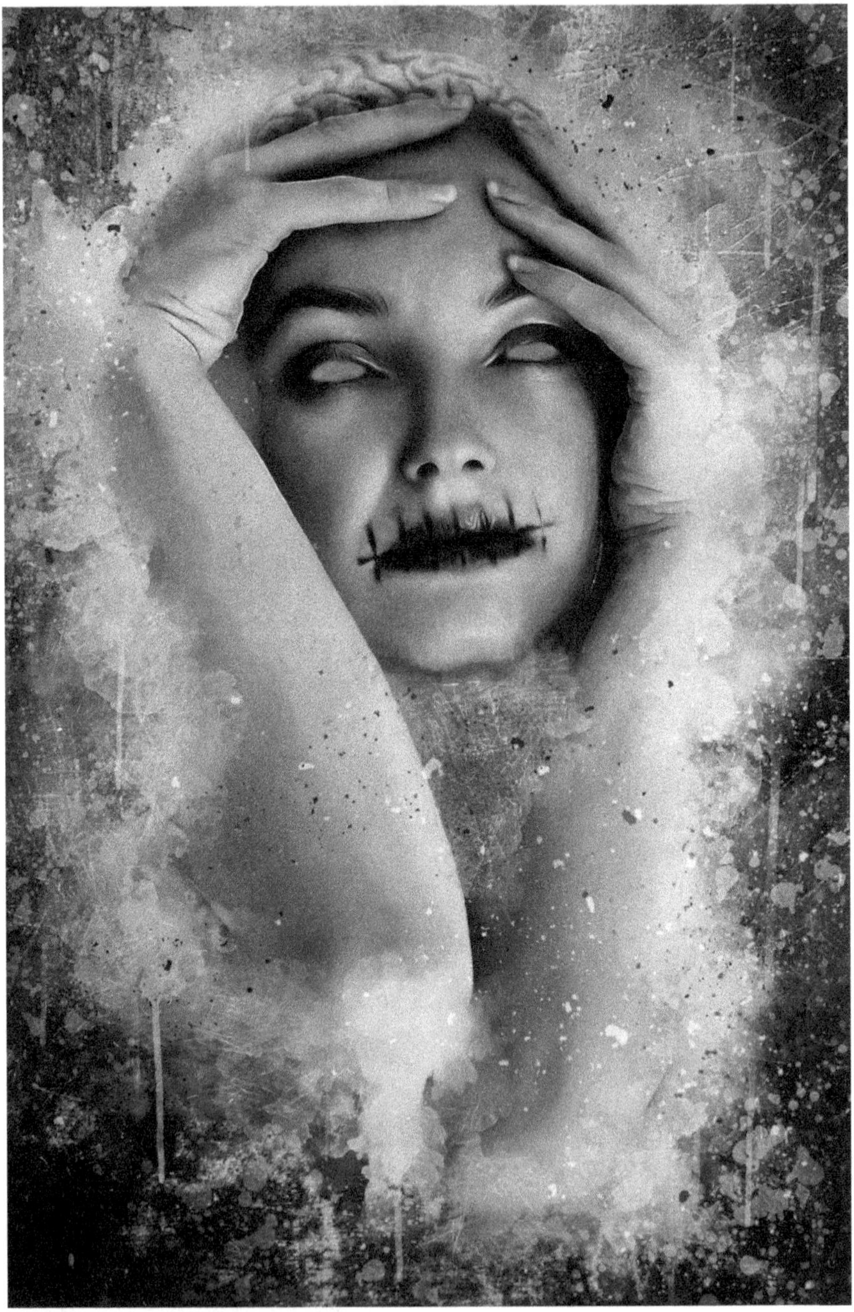

The emotionally needy abuser

This type of abuser often lacks self-esteem and obtains self-worth from relationships – usually romantic ones. They would try to isolate their partner from the outside world and would get very jealous when their partner spends a lot of time with friends or even family. They become very clingy and possessive, and they use manipulation and guilt-tripping as their best tools. If emotional manipulation and abuse aren't working, they resort to physical or verbal abuse just to keep the partner to themselves.

An emotionally needy abuser usually feels like they can't live without their partner. They would make claims such as the partner being their soul mate or that they were meant to be together or even claim that God has revealed to them that they should be together. They would try to convince the partner that there is no other person who would love them the way they do. They are usually consumed with jealousy as well as fear of losing their partner. They make their partner responsible for their happiness. These kinds of abusers are usually hypersensitive, and they cry very easily. Their most preferred love interests are those codependent people who are emotionally stronger than they are and who would be forgiving, doting, and tolerant of them. These abusers can also be verbally, physically, financially, or spiritually abusive.

The addictive abuser

This is an abuser with either one or several addictions. It could be drugs and/or alcohol, sex, gambling, pornography, spending, eating, etc. They are usually ashamed of their addiction(s) and would do anything to hide and cover up their behaviors. These abusers are very skilled at manipulating and lying. Usually, when the addiction involves substance abuse, the abuser is usually volatile and can easily get angered.

Addictive abusers are usually impulsive and seldom exercise self-control. They believe that it is of utmost importance to get their needs and desires met. They enjoy taking risks but sometimes can be reckless. Many times, they would make promises to quit their addiction over and over without following through. However, the best hope for these abusers' is professional long-term treatment. They can also exercise verbal, physical, financial, and spiritual abuse.

The womanizing abuser

A womanizer is usually extremely arrogant and in most cases, unfaithful to their partner. They are excessively consumed with and can even be addicted to seducing and flirting with other women. They are sometimes very charismatic but not all the time.

They derive self-esteem from women or men who reciprocate their advances.

The abuser may or may not be good looking, have very low self-esteem, and they usually claim that they are flirtatious but rather it is just their "personality," so nothing they have done is wrong. They are also expert manipulators and liars who lack any sensitivity towards their partner's hurts, emotions, and needs, and they would rarely validate their partner's feelings.

The womanizing abuser is one that can be defined as a smooth-talker, and they can expertly lie their way out of any situation. This image is very important to them, and sometimes they can resort to blaming their partners for being the unfaithful one instead if they do anything as trivial as wearing lipstick one day. When this blame-game occurs, it could be a sign that they are unfaithful. This abuser normally tends to lack empathy, and they can also be verbally, emotionally, physically, financially, and spiritually abusive.

The chauvinistic abuser

This type of abuser thinks that they are superior, especially in a romantic context. They believe that their rights should always prevail. They lack empathy and compassion and are often very controlling. They can frequently degrade and humiliate their partner without showing any feelings of remorse, would never apologize or admit to any fault.

When confronted, the chauvinistic abuser usually blames their victim for their bad behavior. For example, an abusive husband would claim that if the wife hadn't mouthed-off to him, then he wouldn't have been abusive; therefore, it was his wife's fault. The chauvinistic abuser has many traits that resemble that of a narcissistic abuser. They can also be verbally, emotionally, physically, financially, and spiritually abusive.

The mentally ill abuser

This type of abuser can have mood disorders and even multiple personalities. They can be clinically depressed or may have frequent and unpredictable highs and lows medically known as manic and depressive stages. If the abuser has Obsessive-Compulsive Disorder (OCD) it can cause them to constantly keep tabs on their partner like by calling and texting all the time. Also, they may be anxious, and this can cause them to have a fear of losing their partner or being abandoned.

Other types of mental disorders associated with this type of abuser include borderline personality disorder, bipolar disorder, among others. They can easily be angered or prone to rage, or they can also be hypersensitive and can cry easily. Being on prescribed medication in these situations can sometimes be dangerous, and sometimes when they switch or entirely quit medication, they can be even more dangerous to both themselves and other people.

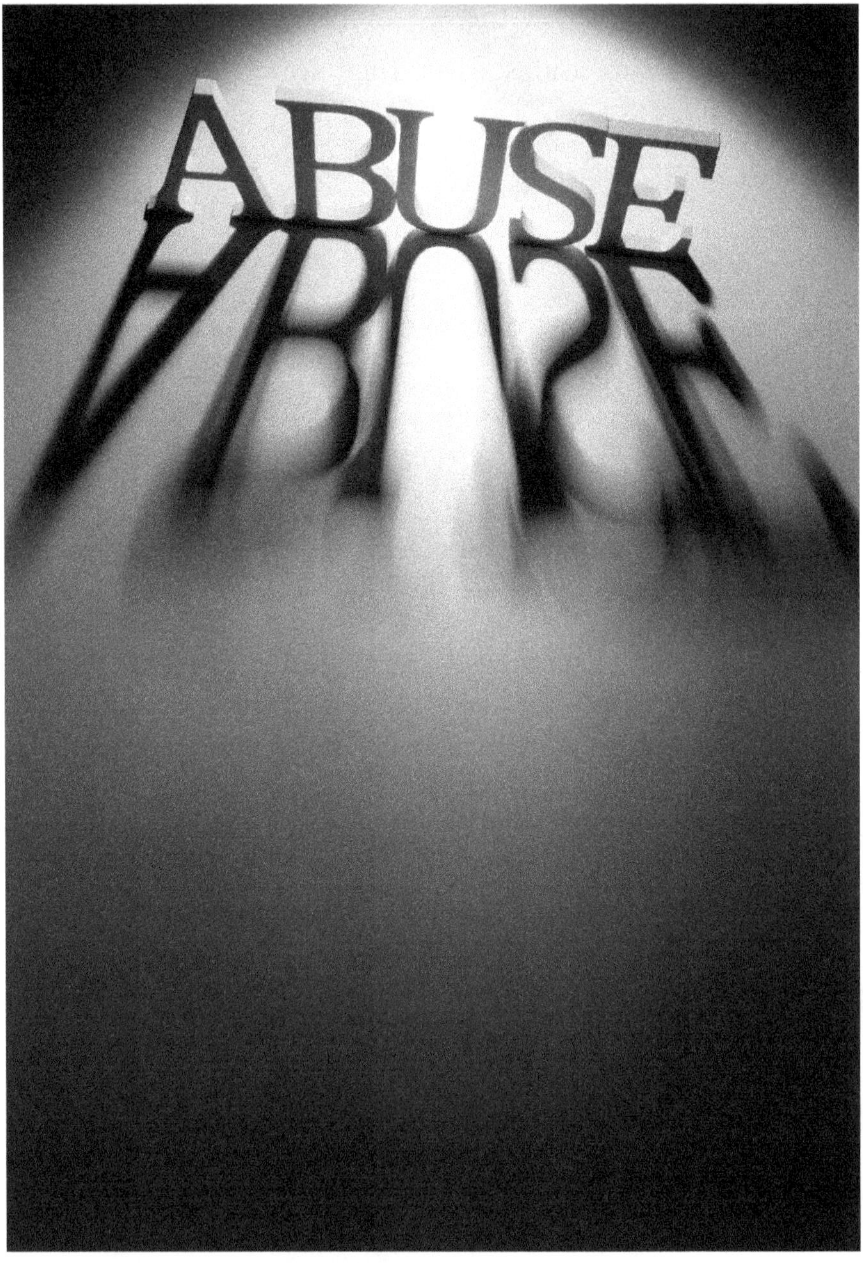
ABUSE

The martyr abuser

The martyr abuser thrives off if sympathy and pity from others and will do anything to be seen as a victim, even lying. This type of abuser may be a child of a mother who highly adored them and constantly excused their bad behavior while growing up. They may even go as far as to threaten suicide or actually attempt to do it in order to gain attention. Most times, they blame other people for their bad behavior. There are also times when they would apologize and claim it won't happen again but would never change or even seek the help they need with the abuse.

The martyr abuser is usually a smooth-talker who can easily persuade anyone into believing them. They are also hypersensitive and would cry easily. They are very emotionally manipulative and abusive and uses guilt-tripping as their greatest tool of manipulation. They can also be physically, verbally, financially, and spiritually abusive.

The perfectionist abuser

The perfectionist abuser demands perfection in other people – especially their partner's in relationships. They are very condescending, impatient, and intolerant at times to other people. They would engage in humiliation and ridicule to get their partner to get them to comply. They are also very critical and would complain regularly about their partner's performance, be it their cooking, cleaning, shopping, driving, parenting, intelligence, work ethic, body weight and even their performance in the bedroom.

The victim is usually left with extremely low self-esteem when abused. The abuser usually also has low self-esteem and degrading other people is usually about making themselves feel good about themselves. They rarely apologize when they are abusive or degrading others. They are also physically, emotionally, verbally, financially, and spiritually abusive.

The misogynistic abuser

This is one of the most dangerous abusive people. A misogynist is a person who despises, dislikes, or is strongly biased against women. There are even religious/Christian persons who hate women. They engage in many tactics to manipulate, control, alienate, isolate, humiliate, destroy, or hurt women, even if they are romantically involved. A misogynist shows no compassion, sympathy, or empathy and couldn't care less when the woman is suffering from like illness and can even deny them medical care at such times. In relationships, they are very controlling, even choosing who the partner can or can't hang out with. To them, a woman's basic job is to serve their men, and they have no value.

A lot of extreme religious cults usually attract this kind of people. If they have any involvement with a religious cult, they would distort the scripture on submission and justify their own bad behaviors. A misogynistic abuser will never admit fault or apologize because they believe they haven't done anything wrong; therefore, the chances of them changing at all are close to nil. These abusers are extremely physically, verbally, emotionally, spiritually, and financially abusive.

The language narcissists use to manipulate their victims

Narcissists are charismatic admirers and lovers of nothing but themselves. If you had fallen for anyone of them before, nobody blames you. Narcissists are experts at making someone feel adored and like the luckiest people in the world before you start being their toy and a slave to their enormous manipulative ego; a victim. They seem to play mind games with a language only they can understand. But this is how you understand it as well.

The soft abuse

This takes place at the beginning of a relationship when neither the victim nor the narcissist has revealed their true colors. The narcissist will use words like "you can trust me." The moment the victim start gaining confidence in them, they serve the narcissists everything, their flaws, past relationships, difficulties, and happy moments. Once they have all this information, they will use it, later on, to provoke and attack them with it.

The myth of eternal love

They are very good at showering their victims with sweet words and promises of eternal love. They would be like "Our love is special" or "I will love you forever." Such words are meant to totally melt the victim's heart and break it later. Once the victim falls for this trap, they become more than happy to follow with the narcissists' manipulative game.

The confusion game

Narcissists would never mean what they say, and at the same time, they would never say what they mean. They are that complicated. They don't like to be criticized or confronted at all; therefore, they will confuse their victims with "I was just joking," "That wasn't what I meant" or "I never said that." Once the victim is left confused and has no clue, they will grab that opportunity to gain power. They always make sure they have the last word.

Using the victim's secrets against them

In the beginning, we mentioned the victim opening up to the narcissists and telling them everything about themselves. Now, this is that time that the narcissists through everything at their victim's face; no mercy! They are experts at using their victim's insecurities and scars of the past against them. They will go like "You are too sensitive" or "You are too needy." They use all the secrets and information to offend the victim. This just goes to show that they have no empathy, and their victim's feelings don't bother them.

Their hidden art of compliments

Narcissists are the best at making a person feel good. Their praises and compliments can take you to the moon and back. But they are false, nothing but a huge deception and lie as well as abusive. "You look nice today, but you looked better yesterday." This is nothing close to honesty. They use a softer voice to criticize their victims for their own sole purposes.

The mirror effect

Narcissists will always find a way to put all the blame on their victims when they know they have wronged. "You are ridiculous" or "stop psychoanalyzing me." These are some of the words they usually say. In the end, the victim will find themselves feeling like they were the ones who did something wrong.

Gaslighting

This is their lethal weapon when they decide and are ready to make their victim feel like they are losing their mind. They automatically become the victim's idol, and the victim is the one seeking approval from them since they seem to know everything. The moment they gain power over their victim, they will start saying accusatory phrases like "You are making that up" or "You are crazy."

In the end, keep in mind that narcissists can either get quiet or loud while using their language. What is important to note is that they will stop at nothing to reach their goals. These people are real psychopaths, and their behavior can lead their victims to depression, anxiety, and even suicide.

Body Language

The same way you train a dog to listen to your body language and cues, you can train a human being to follow you without question. Now there are some people out there who would automatically say that blind obedience is a dangerous thing, this book is not for them. Rather, this book is for those who understand the potential benefits associated with a little absolute control and are willing to do what is required to make that dream a reality.

This won't happen automatically, of course, few things worth having are obtained easily after all, but with practice, you will be able to subtly exert your will on those around you for your own ends. The first step to control those around you lies in analyzing them, however, which is why this chapter will discuss how to analyze people based on their body language.

While initially, you might feel nervous, if you instead make a point of focusing on the body language of those around you and try to pinpoint what type of personality you are dealing with. You might notice the people around you are not exactly at ease, or perhaps some of the people around you seem to be beaming with confidence. You will watch and listen. It is time to train the dog.

Choleric: Generally speaking, you should be able to pick out any cholerics in the room as they are the ones who cannot sit still. If you hope to successfully influence this person, then you are going to need to be prepared to make up for their lack of patience. You can usually hear the choleric person before you see them which is a sign they are in a good mood. It does not take much to get this person's attention because they are happy to give it.

You may find that you have the most difficulty with this personality type as they tend to want to share their passions with others which means they are often naturally charismatic. They may even naturally dominate other personality types, especially phlegmatic individuals which means you are going to need to deal with them first if you are in a group setting. They tend to be natural planners which means they will go along with what you say if you present it as a logical solution to a specific problem.

Another dead giveaway that you are dealing with a choleric person is that they tend to be less emotional than the other personality types. This means they are more likely to be unsympathetic if you play to their emotions and are more likely to be inflexible in general. As such, you will need to appeal to their logic if you hope to make progress. You can use this lack of emotion to your advantage as well, however, as cholerics are often uncomfortable around excessive displays of emotion.

Phlegmatic: On the other side of the scale are the phlegmatic individuals as they are going to be the ones that seem to be the most content with whatever is currently taking place. They will likely be at ease with you or anyone else who approaches them, and you will need to match their wavelength in order to make positive headway with them. One of the best things about phlegmatics is that they are consistent which means that once you convince them to come around to your way of thinking, you won't have to worry about doing it again. They are also naturally affable and prefer to reconcile differences if possible. They are often shy, however, which means they may freeze up if you come at them directly.

Phlegmatic individuals tend to prefer stability to change which means they are often susceptible to ideas that involve remaining with the status quo. As such, if you are ever going to convince them to go against the grain you are going to need to move slowly and get them to understand that they really have no other options. Keep in mind that they can be passive aggressive and don't respond in kind, this is only a response to their dislike of change and is more of an automatic response than anything else.

These types of people often keep their emotions hidden and put forth a relaxed and easy-going façade, regardless of what is going on inside. As such, it is going to take some extra effort to crack their shell and learn how they are really feeling. You may want to engage them in broad conversation to see if you can get a sense of what makes them happy and what makes them angry. Moving forward without this bellwether can be dangerous as it will be difficult to know if they like what you are saying or are opposed to it. While they are often willing to compromise rather than make a scene, they are often quite selfish and will resent any concessions they have to make. Don't forget they have no problem holding grudges.

Melancholic: The melancholic people in the room are likely going to be the ones looking back at you as you look at them. They are the ones who are most likely to be wary of you right off the bat so before you deal with them it is important to plan for resistance. These individuals are often given to deep thought, while still being sensitive to the thoughts and wills of others. This can cause them to focus too much on the innate cruelty in the world which can easily lead to bouts of depression.

One useful trait that most melancholics share is a desire for perfection in all they do which makes them highly conscientious of others. This is directly at odds with the difficulty they often have relating to other people, as they often fail to live up to the melancholic's standards. They are typically very independent and prefer to do things for themselves rather than settling for less than they believe they deserve.

As such, the best way to ingratiate yourself to a melancholic is to appeal to the sense of self-worth that comes along to their perfectionism. If you can find something that allows you access to their ivory tower, then they will naturally be far more inclined to follow your lead; after all, you've proven you have taste. They also only tend to focus on one thing at a time, which means you may need to lead the conversation in order to ensure that it gets to where you need it to be.

Sanguine: Sanguine individuals are known to be charismatic, impulsive and, above all, pleasure-seeking. If you are at a social gathering, then the sanguine individuals will be the loudest ones in the room making friends with everyone else. These personality types often have difficulty following through on tasks, however, which means that a great way to ingratiate yourself to them is by helping them complete the things they totally mean to finish but have not yet gotten around to.

It is very difficult to embarrass a sanguine individual, as they are typically shameless by nature and are always certain that whatever they are doing is the right choice. They are also virtually endless wells of confidence which means you will never make any headway with them by trying to convince them that they have made a wrong move.

They tend to be very physical and enjoy personal contact which means that matching this desire is a great way to score bonus points right out of the gate. They are also naturally curious which means you can also hook them early by showing them something they have never seen before, or at least promising to. They also love to tell stories which means listening and commenting when appropriate is another great ingratiation technique.

The biggest weakness of sanguine individuals is that they tend to feel controlled by their circumstances. As such, if you can convince them that the best way out of the latest situation, they have found themselves in then they will likely go along with whatever it is you are suggesting without a second thought. If you are in a social situation you will want to get them on your side early as they will be more than happy to spread the news of how great you are to everyone else at the party.

What to do with this detail: Knowing the different personality types will help you read people to decide who they really are. From here, you can decide what technique will be needed to persuade them or relax them for your own purposes.

If the other party looks away and down, and then back up at you, take advantage of this opportunity to consider them more closely. This is a sign of vulnerability which means they trust you, so you are free to do with that trust what you may. This is often a good time to ask them about themselves or offer something personal to break the ice. Compliments are always a good choice as it is hard to dislike someone who has recently payed you a compliment.

Smile: The most important asset anyone has is their smile. A smile is a window to the soul. If you are walking down the street and someone gives you a genuine smile, it can change your day. That is the power you want to carry around with you. This is the gift of most sanguine personality types. They are cheerful on the outside and can easily make people laugh. Faking a smile is hard. The truth of any smile lies in the eyes. Pay careful attention to the lines that form when the cheeks rise as the evidence of a genuine smile forms.

If you ask someone to do something and they decline, smile anyway, they will feel bad for saying no. Depending on their actual reaction, say it again in a different way and in a cartoonish voice (humor), and follow up with a serious voice. Ask for the favor again by adding another smile. This is best used in social situations and is to be avoided at work. Unless you are super cool with your co-workers or if you are sure you are dealing with a sanguine personality.

If your co-worker or your boss display a dislike for emotions or seem impatient, you could be dealing with a choleric personality. You will need to make it seem like they are the leaders. You're pushing boundaries, but you don't want anyone to recognize this game. No matter how it ends, do not give too much of a reaction. If you are too happy, it could kill the vibe. The same is true if you are too upset, just smile. You will not be able to change your own personality type as the theory is that you were born that way. However, knowing more about yourself, you can control the display, or even master your weaknesses to have influence or get close enough to other people, that you may sincerely analyze them.

Negative personality cues

Now that you have a basic understanding of positive body language, let us look at the opportunity to dig into the negative cues often given by different personality types. Sometimes even the most trustworthy and genuine people can give off signals of distress through body cues, so it is important to take them with a grain of salt to avoid being misled.

If you find someone who is trying to discourage you, or they are judging you, it is likely that their personality is phlegmatic If the negativity you are picking up on is coming from someone who is demanding attention or seems phony, you are amidst a sanguine personality type. You want to know the difference and how to respond to either situation to achieve a goal. Whether it is to cheer someone up, so you can enjoy their company or perhaps you need to get away from someone who would seek to destroy your aura. Either way, practice makes perfect, and observing takes a lot of it.

Personal space: If someone moves away from you, this is often a sign that they believe you either did something wrong or you represent something negative to them. This mentality applies to all four of the personality types. It hurts to feel rejected. Instead of feeling sorry for yourself, move back into their realm if you want to change the vibe.

Your sanguine personality types will not move away from you. They like to be close to the person they are listening to. Do not let this throw you off. Insist that you are worth it. Don't say it, but simply adjust your posture to a very relaxed position. You can do this by pointing your feet at that person, smiling and either asking a question about their job or what city they are from. From here, still smiling, ask if they want to get some fresh air. You have now created an intimate moment with someone who wasn't so sure about you. Let your sanguine personality do a lot of the talking if they do walk out the door with you as there is a good chance they will take a walk with you because they are restless.

Defuse a negative situation: If you need to stay cool until you can make an exit in a tough situation, avoid smiling. This occurs where someone is giving the impression that they are unstable or unsafe. Although, they are likely to be sanguine personality which is also known for turning people off, try to distinguish if they are angry or actually going to zap you of your will to live. What you need to do is avoid staring at the person but to make a few seconds of eye contact and act like everything is fine. This is an extreme example, but if someone had a gun to your head, you do not want to freak out and cry. Rather, you would want to stay calm, cool, and collected. This is the strength of a phlegmatic personality type.

Crying and carrying on, would irritate the person and they might lose their cool and shoot you. This could happen if they are a choleric personality type, which has an extreme distaste for tears and is unsympathetic towards other in general. in intense situations as it tends to make people a little calmer and more likely to bend to your will.

Looking side to side: Whether in a social setting or a professional setting, whoever you are dealing with should not be looking side to side. This means they are uncomfortable or bored. Are they coming across as guarded? A melancholic personality type may seem guarded when they are truly just in their own world. If you are confronted with this situation, use the opportunity to display positive body language to gain control of the vibe.

Conclusion

If you have never been creative in your life and you were suddenly told that it was possible to be creative, you would probably dismiss this thought because your mind is programmed to believe that you are not creative. Tap into the subconscious and learn how much creativity lurks within that place you underestimate. It's amazing where this journey will take you.

Grab a notebook and a pen and set aside quality time each day to do this for yourself. You can work NLP technique into any schedule and see positive results pretty fast. Each step is easy to understand and do. Before you know it, you can have the problem isolated and put a plan of action in place that creates the lasting change you desire.

There are many types of behavior modification therapy available. They all work to some degree, but it is the time and expense involved that can be frustrating. Most traditional behavior modification therapies include time-intensive programs that cost you and your insurance company a lot of money over time. NLP works the same way, but it brings you to the results faster without the expense.

If you have some behaviors that you would like to change or want to enjoy a more stable emotional wellbeing NLP offers you all of the benefits of intense therapy without the hassle and high cost. You now have all of the tools at your access to get started right away. Make this the day that you finally took control of your life and got the edge!

Use empathy and learn how empathy works to communicate with others by suggestion rather than by giving definite answers that cut other people's hopes and dreams down in size. There is no need to belittle. In fact, you grow richer from learning to use empathy because you become a better person for it and are able to make friendships that benefit everyone involved.

Learn not to limit yourself by believing in things that are limiting in themselves. An example recently read was where a person believed that birds all have feathers. It's something that limits the believer, since by that premise penguins would be excluded. What NLP does is help you to see a much bigger picture that doesn't limit what you see and that's when your life begins to take on a whole new meaning.

It is hoped that this book has opened your mind to the possibility of taking your learning processes further on the subject of NLP. You will be very glad that you did, as the techniques briefly outlined in this book, have vast potential.

CPSIA information can be obtained
at www.ICGtesting.com
Printed in the USA
BVHW062035010321
601387BV00007B/612

9 781801 860994